WAVERLEY
BOOKS

Published 2010 by Waverley Books,
144 Port Dundas Road, Glasgow, G4 0HZ

Copyright © Scottish Dementia Working Group 2010

Cartoons inside and on the cover drawn by Edward McLaughlin,
Chair Scottish Dementia Working Group

The font used in this book is FS Me – a font designed to aid legibility for those
with learning disability. FS Me was researched and developed in conjunction with – and
endorsed by – Mencap, the UK's leading charity and voice for those with
learning disability. Mencap receive a donation for each font licence purchased.

A catalogue entry for this book is available from the British Library

ISBN 978-1-84934-013-7

Printed and bound in the UK

Contents

Contents

Introduction   9

Doctor, doctor   13

Suffer the
little children   27

Those golden years   31

Spots before your eyes   39

The loot of all evil?   41

Waiter!   45

Mars and Venus   49

Born to shop   57

To travel hopefully   61

Nice work   65

Teeing off   75

The best days of your life   79

Animal magic   85

Kids' jokes   89

A slight technical hitch   101

A man walks into a bar ...   111

Saints and sinners 115

Church clangers 121

Strong arm of the law 129

Cannibal capers 139

No laughing matter 143

The Rovers 147

Quiz time 151

Lucky dip 163

Murphy's lesser-known laws 171

About SDWG 175

Acknowledgements 192

Introduction

The Scottish Dementia Working Group was formed in 2002 by a group of people with dementia who wanted to speak for ourselves. Since then we have become highly successful in our campaign to improve services for people with dementia and to improve attitudes towards people with dementia.

In October 2007, fifteen of our members took part in a workshop on the subject of "Humour and Dementia". This may seem an odd topic to address, as dementia is not viewed as a laughing matter by those affected by it. On the other hand, paradoxically, humour can be a very powerful means of coping in difficult circumstances.

At the end of the workshop, we came up with ideas for using humour constructively, including producing a book of jokes which could help break down some of the fear the condition instils.

So this is it. Read on …. and don't forget to laugh!

For more information about the SDWG, see our website: **www.sdwg.org.uk**

Freephone Dementia Helpline: **0808 808 3000**

Doctor, doctor

Arriving home one evening, a man finds his pregnant wife in labour, so he phones the hospital.

"My wife is having contractions and they're only two minutes apart, tell me what should I do?" he asks frantically.

"Is this her first child?" asks the doctor.

"No, you fool," the man shouts, "this is her husband!" *Ed*

An elderly gentleman went to the doctor complaining of deafness. The doctor had him fitted for a hearing aid that allowed the man to hear perfectly.

The next time the doctor saw his patient, he said, "Your hearing is perfect. Your family must be really pleased that you can hear again."

The man replied, "Oh, I haven't told my family yet. I just sit around and listen to the conversations. I've changed my will three times!" *Ed*

I asked my doctor, "Have you got anything to keep my hair in?"

He gave me a shoebox.

Ed

Doctor: "How did you manage to burn both ears?"

Patient: "Well, I was doing the ironing and the phone rang, and I answered the iron by mistake. When I put the phone down and clutched my sore ear, it rang again."

James

"Doctor, doctor, I swallowed the film from my camera."

"Well, we'll just have to wait and see what develops."

James

"Doctor, doctor, I think I'm a pair of curtains."

"For heaven's sake pull yourself together." *James*

I went to my doctor and asked for something for persistent wind.

He gave me a kite. *Les Dawson; sent in by Ed*

"Doctor, doctor, I feel like a spoon."

"Sit there and don't stir!" *Kath and Isobel*

"Doctor, doctor, I think I'm a bridge!"

"What's come over you?"

"Two cars, a truck and a coach."   *Kath and Isobel*

A patient was coming round from an operation.
He was in quite an agitated state and told the
recovery nurse that he had heard the surgeon utter
a four-letter word during the operation.

"What did he say?" she asked.

"Oops," he replied.   *James*

"Doctor, doctor, I'm a kleptomaniac!"

"Take these pills and if that doesn't work,
pick me up a DVD player!"   *Kath and Isobel*

"Doctor, doctor, I swallowed my pillow last night."

"How do you feel now?"

"Oh, just a little down in the mouth."   *James*

"Doctor, doctor, I think I'm a bell."

"Well, if it persists give me a ring."   *James*

"Doctor, doctor, I think I'm a pack of cards."

"I'll deal with you later."   *James*

Mother (on phone): "Doctor, come quickly, the baby has swallowed my biro pen."

Doctor: "Stay calm and I'll be right over. What are you doing meantime?"

Mother: "Using a pencil." *James*

———————————

"Doctor, doctor, people treat me like a wheelbarrow."

"Well, don't let them push you around." *James*

———————————

"Doctor, doctor, I think I'm shrinking."

"You'll just have to be a little patient." *James*

Nurse: "Doctor, there's an invisible man in the waiting room."

Doctor: "Tell him I can't see him."   *James*

A man went into the chemist's and asked for a cure for hiccups. The chemist slapped him and said, "There, you don't have hiccups any more, do you?"

"No," said the man, "but my wife still has."   *James*

Did you hear about the constipated accountant?

He couldn't budget.   *James*

A man goes to the doctor complaining that every part of his body hurts no matter where he touches it.

The doctor examines him and says, "I know the problem — you've broken your finger."   *James*

"Incontinence hotline. Can you hold, please?"   *James*

Did you hear about the constipated mathematician?

He worked it out with a pencil.   *James*

Did you hear about the man who fell into an upholstery machine?

He is now fully recovered. *James*

Did you hear about the constipated composer?

He couldn't finish his last movement. *James*

A doctor was instructing his students around the autopsy table. "This is the liver, this is the heart, these are the kidneys," he intoned.

"What's happening?" whispered a late arrival.

"He's doing an organ recital," said her friend. *James*

A man went to his doctor complaining of
a sore stomach.

After an examination, the doctor said,
"I can't find anything. It must be the drink."

"OK," the man said, "I'll come back when you're sober."

James

A psychiatrist congratulated his patient on the
progress he had made.

"You call this progress!" shouted the patient.
"Six months ago I was Napoleon and now
I'm a nobody."

Ed

A psychiatrist received a postcard from one
of his patients who was on holiday.

"Having a lovely time," it read. "Why?"

Ed

Psychiatrist: "What is the opposite of sadness?"

Patient: "Joy."

Psychiatrist: "What is the opposite of depressed?"

Patient: "Lively."

Psychiatrist: "What is the opposite of woe?"

Patient: "Giddy up."

James

Getting older: the new alphabet

A's for arthritis;

B's the bad back;

C's the chest pains — perhaps cardiac?

D is for dental decay and decline;

E is for eyesight, can't read that top line!

F is for fissures and fluid retention;

G is for gas which I'd rather not mention!

H is high blood pressure — I'd rather it low;

I's for incisions with scars you can show.

J is for joints, out of socket, won't mend,

K is for knees that crack when they bend.

L's for libido, what happened to sex?

M is for memory, I forget what comes next.

N's for neuralgia, in nerves way down low;

O is for osteo, the bones that don't grow!

P's for prescriptions, I have quite a few;
Just give me a pill and I'll be good as new!

Q is for queasy, is it fatal or flu?

R is for reflux, one meal turns to two.

S is for sleepless nights, counting my fears,

T is for tinnitus: there are bells in my ears!

U is for urinary; big troubles with flow.

V is for vertigo, that's "dizzy", you know.

W is for worry, now what's going round?

X is for X-ray, and what might be found.

Y is for another year I'm left here behind,

Z is for zest that I still have – in my mind.

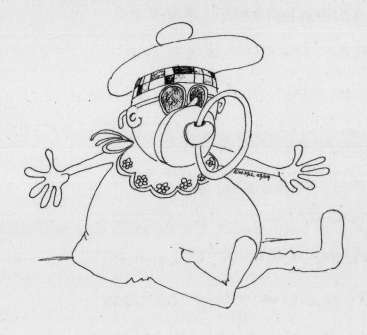

Suffer the
little children

Two aunts were minding their four-year-old niece, who was watching television.

One said to the other, "What a pity that she isn't very P-R-E-T-T-Y."

The little girl turned round and said, "It doesn't matter, so long as I am C-L-E-V-E-R."   *Ed*

A youngster asks what time is it.

"Three thirty," a passerby replies.

"Strange, I've been asking the time all day and each time I get a different answer."   *James*

I was packing for my business trip and my three-year-old daughter was having a wonderful time playing on the bed.

At one point she said, "Daddy, look at this," and stuck out two of her fingers.

Trying to keep her entertained, I reached out and stuck her tiny fingers in my mouth and said, "Daddy's gonna eat your fingers," pretending to eat them.

I went back to packing, looked up again and my daughter was standing on the bed staring at her fingers with a devastated look on her face. I said, "What's wrong, honey?"

She replied, "What happened to my bogey?"   *Ed*

Did you hear about the teenager who got AM radio? It took ages before he realised he could play it in the afternoon.   *James*

A boy took his pal to visit his granny. While talking to her, his friend munched through an entire bowl of peanuts.

"You've eaten all the nuts!" accused the first boy.

"Never mind," said the granny, "I did manage to suck all the chocolate off them earlier."

James

A teenager came through from the kitchen looking puzzled. "I don't know what happened," she said. "I just washed some ice cubes for the drinks but I can't find them now."

James

Teenager to his friend: "I don't really like having orange spiky hair shaved at the sides, a nose ring and torn clothes, but it stops my parents taking me anywhere."

James

Those golden years

Anyone can get old. All you have to do is
live long enough.

Groucho Marx

Old age is when you've met so many people that every
new person you meet reminds you of someone else.

Ogden Nash; sent in by Ed

A couple in their nineties were both having problems
remembering things. During a check-up, the doctor
told them that they were physically OK, but they
might want to start writing things down to help
them remember. Later that night, while watching TV,
the old man got up from his chair. "Want anything
while I'm in the kitchen?" he asked.

"Will you get me a bowl of ice cream?"

"OK."

"Don't you think you should write it down so you can remember it?" she asked.

"No, I can remember it."

"Well, I'd like some strawberries on top, too. Maybe you should write it down, so you don't forget it?"

He said, "I can remember that. You want a bowl of ice cream with strawberries."

"I'd also like whipped cream. I'm certain you'll forget that, why don't you write it down?" she said.

Irritated, he said, "I don't need to write it down, I can remember it! Ice cream with strawberries and whipped cream — I can remember that, for goodness sake!"

Off he went into the kitchen. After about twenty minutes, he came back from the kitchen and handed his wife a plate of bacon and eggs. She stared at the plate for a moment.

"Where's my toast?"

Ed

At the age of 82, Hamish went to the doctor for a check-up.

A few days later, the doctor saw Hamish walking down the street with a beautiful young woman on his arm.

Shortly afterwards the doctor saw Hamish again and said, "You're really doing well, aren't you?"

Hamish replied, "Just doing what you said, Doctor: 'Get a hot mamma and be cheerful.'"

The doctor said, "I didn't say that. I said, 'You've got a heart murmur — be careful!'"   *Ed*

––––––––––

Middle age is when you go on holiday and pack a sweater.   *Denis Norden; sent in by Ed*

Three folks with dementia share a house together.

Jimmy is upstairs running a bath. Bath full, he swings over to get in. "Och," he says, "I can't mind if I was getting into this bath or getting out of it."

He shouts downstairs, "Jackie, do you know if I was getting into this bath or out of it?"

Jackie goes up the stairs. Halfway up the stair he stops. "Gee, I can't remember if I was going up these stairs or down them."

He shouts downstairs, "Heather, do you know if I was going up the stairs or down them?"

Heather's sitting in the kitchen. "Gee, I'm glad I don't have memory problems like those two. Touch wood." She knocks on the table.

"Who's at the door?" she asks.　　　　　　*Ian Hewines*

Three elderly guys were out walking.

The first one said, "Windy, isn't it?"

The second one said, "No, it's Thursday!"

The third one said, "So am I. Let's go and get a beer." *Ed*

Two elderly ladies had been friends for many decades. Over the years they had shared all kinds of activities and adventures. Lately, their activities had been limited to meeting a few times a week to play cards.

One day they were playing cards when one looked at the other and said, "Now don't get mad at me. I know we've been friends for a long time... but I just can't think of your name! I've thought and thought, but I can't remember it. Please tell me what your name is."

Her friend glared at her. For at least three minutes she just sat and glared at her. Finally she said, "How soon do you need to know?"

Chris McGregor, Vice-Convener, Alzheimer Scotland

Two pensioners were sitting on a bench enjoying the spring sunshine when one turned to the other and asked, "Hey Joe, do you remember the last time you went out with a woman?"

"Yes," replied Joe without hesitation, "it must have been about nineteen thirty."

"Gee, that was a long time ago," his friend sympathised.

"Not really, it's only twenty hundred now," answered Joe, looking at his watch.

The Rovers, Alzheimer Scotland, South Aberdeenshire Services

———————————

A man was telling his neighbour, "I've just bought a new hearing aid. It cost me four thousand pounds, but it's state-of-the-art. It's perfect."

"Really," answered the neighbour. "What kind is it?"

"Twelve thirty."

Ed

An elderly couple had dinner at another couple's house and, after eating, the wives left the table and went into the kitchen.

The two men were talking and one said, "Last night we went out to a new restaurant and it was really great. I would recommend it very highly."

The other man said, "What is the name of the restaurant?"

The first man thought and thought and finally said, "What is the name of that flower you give to someone you love? You know... The one that's red and has thorns."

"Do you mean a rose?"

"Yes, that's the one," replied the man. He turned towards the kitchen and yelled, "Rose, what's the name of that restaurant we went to last night?"   *Ed*

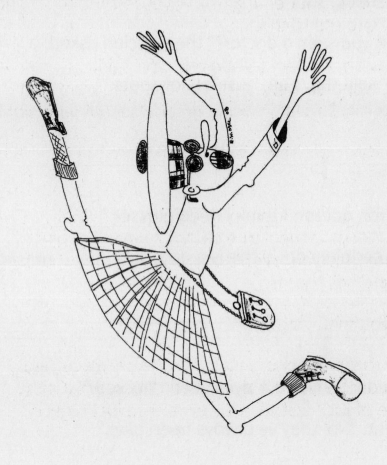

Spots before your eyes

In aid of the SDWG supported by Comic Relief and Alzheimer Scotland

A man went to the optician and complained that he kept seeing spots.

"Have you seen a doctor?" the optician asked.

"No," said the man, "just lots of spots."

James

"Doctor, doctor, I think I need glasses."

"You certainly do — this is a garage!"

Kath and Isobel

Optician: "Have your eyes been checked?"

Patient: "No, they've always been blue."

James

The loot of all evil?

A man walked into a bank and asked to cash a cheque.

The cashier said, "Yes, that's fine, but you'll have to identify yourself."

The man took out a mirror, looked into it, and said, "Yes, that's me all right!"

Ed

———————

A toff was riding in his Rolls Royce when he saw two men eating grass at the roadside. He told his driver to stop and ask what they were doing. They said they were penniless and hungry, so the toff asked them to come home with him. They said how grateful they were.

"Nonsense," the toff replied, "my grass is three feet high at my mansion and I could do with the help."

James

A man went to the bank and asked the cashier
to check his balance.

So she pushed him.   *James*

Tom: "I wish I had enough money to buy a Rolls Royce."

Pat: "Why do you want a Rolls Royce?"

Tom: "I don't, I just wish I had the money."   *James*

One of the shortest wills ever written:
"Being of a sound mind, I spent all my money."   *Ed*

In aid of the SDWG supported by Comic Relief and Alzheimer Scotland

A woman went to the bank to cash a birthday cheque from her husband.

"You'll have to endorse it," the teller said.

"Oh," she said, and wrote "My husband is a generous man."

James

Waiter!

In aid of the SDWG supported by Comic Relief and Alzheimer Scotland

A woman goes into a new coffee shop in Partick and asks for a coffee.

When it arrives she says, "Where's the free wiffy?"

"I don't know what you mean," says the waiter.

"It says outside, coffee and free wiffy."

"Oh," he replied, "You mean Wi-Fi."

A true story sent in by Pauline McNeill, MSP

"Waiter," said the customer, "there's a hair in this honey."

"Ah," replied the waiter, "it must be from the comb!" *Ed*

Definition of a hotel: a place which keeps the manufacturers of 25-watt bulbs in business. *James*

One of our ladies is on the drug trial for TauRx Therapeutics Ltd, and while on holiday in Spain she was called to the hotel reception.

She was asked why she felt it necessary to bring her own cleaning products on holiday, and were the hotel's standards unacceptable?

The lady explained that the blue in the loo was the side-effect of the drug and it is hard to flush away.

Alzheimer Scotland, Aberdeen City Services, Drop In

A group of chess enthusiasts are standing in a hotel lobby discussing tournament victories.

After an hour, the manager comes by and asks them to go to their rooms.

"But why?" they ask, as they move off.

"Because," he says, "I can't stand chess nuts boasting in an open foyer."

James

Mars and Venus

Wife: "The two best things I can cook are stew and apple pie."

Husband: "Which is this?"   *Ed*

_____

Here comes the bride

Short fat and wide,

She how she wobbles from side to side.

Here comes the groom,

All full of gloom,

He's thin as a broom

Going to meet his doom.   *James*

Definition of a silver wedding: the occasion during which the happy couple celebrate that twenty-five years are over.

James

One hot day a woman walked into the kitchen to find her husband swatting flies.

"Have you managed to get any?" she asked.

"Oh, yes," he replied, "three males and two females."

"How can you tell?" she said.

"Well," he said, "three were on the beer and two were on the phone."

Ed

Eve to Adam on St Valentine's Day: "Do you love only me?"

Adam to Eve: "Who else?!"

Ed

A man is standing on the bathroom scales holding his stomach in.

"That won't help," his wife remarks.

"Yes it will," he says, "it's the only way to read the numbers."

James

Wife: "What is my favourite flower?"

Husband (not paying attention): "...Er, um ...self-raising?"

Chris McGregor, Vice-Convener, Alzheimer Scotland

A man was griping in the bar: "I had it all — fast car, a big house and the love of a beautiful woman."

"What happened?" asked the barman.

"My wife found out."

James

I accidentally left the fridge door open and all the food went off.

My wife was furious. "What am I supposed to do with all this food!"

I said, "Look love, don't make a meal out of it."   *James*

———————————

Husband: "I got an anonymous letter today."

Wife: "Really? Who was it from?"   *James*

———————————

A wife yelled at her husband: "You're going to be sorry! I'm going to leave you!"

"Make up your mind," said her husband.
"Which is it going to be?"   *James*

A woman ran into her house one Saturday shouting to her husband to pack his stuff as she had won the lottery.

"Shall I pack for hot or cold weather?" he asked.

"Whatever," she said, "as long as you are gone in the morning."

James

Q: What do you call a woman who knows where her husband is every night?

A: A widow.

Chris McGregor, Vice-Convener, Alzheimer Scotland

A man went to the florist's to buy his wife anemones, but all that was left were some green leaves.

He bought the foliage and was delighted when she said, "With fronds like these who needs anemones?"

James

After forty years of marriage, a millionaire changed his will, leaving everything to his wife if she remarried when he died.

"Why do that?" asked his lawyer.

"Well, I just want someone to be sorry that I died."

James

––––––––––––––––––

A man took his dog to the vet and asked for its tail to be cut off.

"Why?" asked the vet.

"Well, my mother-in-law is coming tomorrow and I don't want anyone making her feel welcome." *James*

A woman was looking out of her window watching her neighbour's husband.

She told her husband, "He kisses his wife on the doorstep every day when he goes out. Why don't you do that?"

"I hardly know her," he replied.

James

A couple were sitting in a café and suddenly the man slid under the table.

"Excuse me," said the waitress, "I think your husband is ill, he just slid under the table."

"No," said the woman, "he just walked in the door."

James

Born to shop

In the days of the US Polaris base in the Holy Loch, a Dunoon shopkeeper got a trial consignment of disposable underpants in packs of six and twelve. He put them on display to see if they would sell. A submariner from the US base came in, saw the disposable underpants and asked for fourteen.

"Why fourteen?" asked the shopkeeper. "They come in packs of six and twelve."

"I'm going on a two-week tour of duty," replied the American. "Fourteen would be the right number."

The pants hadn't been selling well so the shopkeeper agreed to break open a pack and sell him fourteen. After doing this, he realised that packs of seven and fourteen would make more sense for people going on holidays or duty tours. He broke open all the remaining packs and resealed them in packs of seven and fourteen. Just then, a local farmer came in, saw the disposable underpants and asked for a packet of twelve.

"Why do you want a packet of twelve?" asked the exasperated shopkeeper. "I've just rearranged them into packs of seven and fourteen."

"Well," replied the farmer, "I need one for January, one for February..."   *Donald Lyons, Director, Mental Welfare Commission*

A man goes into the butcher's and says,
"Have you got pig's feet?"

"Yes," says the butcher.

"Well, can you trot over and get me some?"   *James*

A woman walked into a butcher's shop and asked
for a chicken. The butcher brought her his last one.

"It's too small," she said. "Have you a larger one?"

So he took it into the back shop, plumped it up, and
brought it back.

"That's great," said the lady, "I'll just take both now."

James

My girlfriend will buy anything marked down.
In a store last week she bought an escalator.   *James*

––––––––––––––––––

Bob: "I was at a jumble sale today and bought a carpet in mint condition."

Jim: "What do you mean it was in mint condition?"

Bob: "It has a hole in the middle."   *James*

To travel hopefully

Sign on rear of car:

"If you can read this, I've lost my caravan." *Ed*

A glue tanker on the motorway has shed its load.

Drivers are advised to stick to the inside lane. *James*

Policeman: "I'm arresting you for speeding.
You were doing at least 100 miles an hour."

Motorist: "That's nonsense, officer, I've only been
driving ten minutes." *James*

A policeman stopped a driver and, after checking his papers, said, "It says here you're supposed to wear glasses."

"But I have contacts," protested the driver.

"I don't care who you know," snapped the officer. "You're breaking the law."

James

A couple from a dry country were travelling in a train with a Russian man named Rudolph. The man looked out of the window and said, "It is sleeting."

"Not so," said Rudolph. "It is raining."

They argued for ages, until the wife said to her husband, "Surely you know that Rudolph the Red knows rain, dear?"

James

Q: What would happen if everyone had a pink car?

A: We'd be a pink car-nation.   *James*

Tom: "I've been driving cars for thirty years without an accident."

Pat: "I suppose I could call you a wreckless driver." *James*

Nice work

An employer reprimanded his newest recruit. "You're half an hour late every day. Don't you know when we start work in this office?"

"No sir," he replied, "everyone is busy working when I arrive."

James

Q: Why is Christmas just like a day at the office?

A: You do all the work and the plump guy in the suit gets all the credit.

James

A man driving along a country road saw a farmer standing still in his field.

"What are you doing?" he shouted.

The farmer replied, "I'm trying to win a Nobel Prize for being out standing in my field."

James

A man went to see a harassed circus ringmaster.
"I have this very original act," said the man,
"I do bird impressions."

The ringmaster looked at him with incredulity.
"Bird impressions! They went out with Queen Victoria,
I am too busy for this nonsense, away you go, beat it."

"But this is diff—" said the man.

"No!" interrupted the ringmaster, blood pressure rising.
"I have heard enough, begone or else!"

"OK," the man said and flapping his arms he flew
out of the window.　　　　　　　　　　　　　　*James*

———————————

Q: What do you call an unemployed court jester?

A: Nobody's fool.　　　　　　　　　　　　　　　*James*

Did you hear about the woman who started
a bonsai nursery?

She was so successful, she moved into
smaller premises.   *James*

The human cannonball decided to quit the circus.
The ringmaster was furious and yelled, "Where am
I supposed to find someone of your calibre?"   *James*

The recruit was doing push-ups in the driving rain.

The drill sergeant said, "I bet you can't wait to spit
on my grave."

"Oh no," said the recruit, "when I am discharged,
I am never standing in line again."   *James*

A dry-cleaner's business was running a new advertising campaign: "Guaranteed clean in 24 hours". A man, seeing this, went in with a coat, asking that it be done in 24 hours. As he was leaving, he was a bit worried to see that the assistant threw the coat in a large pile in the corner. Returning the next day, he saw the coat still lying in the same pile.

"No, the coat is not ready," admitted the assistant. "While we guarantee 24-hour cleaning, we're never very sure which 24 hours we're talking about!"

Tavish Scott, MSP

Two businessmen were discussing a mutual acquaintance.

"I put him back on his feet," boasted one.

"How did you do that?" the other asked.

"I repossessed his car."

James

An older couple had a son who was still living with his parents. They were a little worried, as the son was still unable to decide about his future career; so they decided to do a small test. They took a ten pound note, a Bible and a bottle of whisky, and put them on the hall table. Then they hid, pretending they were not at home.

The father said to his wife, "If our son takes the money, he will be a businessman. If he takes the Bible, he will be a priest — but if he takes the bottle of whisky, I'm afraid our son will be a drunkard."

So the parents hid in the nearby cupboard and waited nervously.

Peeping through the keyhole, they saw their son arrive. He picked up the ten pound note, looked at it against the light, and slid it into his pocket. After that, he took the Bible, flicked through it, and pocketed it. Finally he grabbed the bottle, opened it, and took an appreciative whiff to be assured of the quality... then he went upstairs, carrying all three items.

The father slapped his forehead, and said: "Oh no! It's even worse than I could ever have imagined — our son is going to be a politician!"

Irene Oldfather, MSP

A mechanic was removing the cylinder heads from the motor of a car when he spotted a famous heart surgeon in his shop, standing at the side, waiting for the service manager to come and take a look at his car.

The mechanic shouted across the garage, "Hello Doctor! Please come over here for a minute."

The famous surgeon, a bit surprised, walked over to the mechanic.

The mechanic straightened up, wiped his hands on a rag and asked argumentatively, "So, doctor, look at this. I also open hearts, take valves out, grind them, put in new parts, and when I finish this will work as good as new. So how come you get the big money, when you and me are doing basically the same work?"

The doctor leaned over and whispered to the mechanic: "Try doing it when the engine is running."

Chris McGregor, Vice-Convener, Alzheimer Scotland

Two businessmen were discussing a mutual acquaintance.

"I put him back on his feet," boasted one.

"How did you do that?" the other asked.

"I repossessed his car."

James

———————————

An architect, a surgeon and an economist are discussing the Creation.

The surgeon says: "Look, we surgeons are most important. God's a surgeon, because the first thing he did was to extract Eve from Adam's rib."

The architect says: "No, wait a minute, God is an architect. He made the world in seven days out of chaos."

The economist smiles: "And who made the chaos?"

Robert Brown, MSP

Tom was being interviewed for a job and was asked why he had left his previous work.

"I got sacked for playing with the bacon slicer," he said.

"Surely that wasn't considered a sacking offence?" the interviewer asked.

"It must have been," said Tom. "They sacked her too."

James

The recruit was doing push-ups in the driving rain.

The drill sergeant said, "I bet you can't wait to spit on my grave."

"Oh no," said the recruit, "when I am discharged, I am never standing in line again."

James

Recruiting sergeant: "So you want to join the army —
what's your name, son?"

Recruit: "Fish."

Recruiting sergeant: "Right, we'll put you in
the tank regiment." *James*

Teeing off

A golfer was thrashing vainly away at the ball.
"I'd move heaven and earth to reach 90," he said.

"Try heaven," said his partner. "You've moved
enough earth already."

James

―――――――――――――

A golfer was having problems.

"You're standing too close to the ball,"
his partner explained. "After you've hit it."

James

―――――――――――――

A golfer was taking ages teeing off. "My wife is
watching me from the clubhouse," he explained.
"I want to make it a perfect shot."

"Don't be silly," his partner said. "You'll never hit
her from here."

James

"Why don't you play golf with Jim any more?"
the golfer's wife asked.

"Well, would you play with someone who cheats and
lies about his handicap?" answered her husband.

"No," she said.

"Well, neither will Jim."

James

_____

Did you know that when a woman wears a leather
dress, a man's heart beats quicker, his throat gets dry,
he gets weak in the knees, and he begins to
think irrationally?

Ever wonder why?

It's because she smells like a new golf bag!

James

A golfer came home to be greeted by his little boy:
"Did you win today, Daddy?"

"Well, not quite, son, but I did get to hit the ball
a lot more than the others."   *James*

The best days
of your life

Teacher: George Washington not only chopped down his father's cherry tree, but also admitted it. Now, Louie, do you know why his father didn't punish him?

Louie: Because George still had the axe in his hand.

Agnes

_____

Teacher: Now, Simon, tell me frankly, do you say prayers before eating?

Simon: No, I don't have to, my Mum is a good cook.

Agnes

_____

Teacher: John, why are you doing your maths multiplication on the floor?

John: You told me to do it without using tables.   *Agnes*

Teacher: Donald, what is the chemical formula for water?

Donald: HIJKLMNO.

Teacher: What are you talking about?

Donald: Yesterday you said it's H to O.   *Agnes*

_____

Teacher: Maria, go to the map and find North America.

Maria: Here it is.

Teacher: Correct. Now class, who discovered America?

Class: Maria.   *Agnes*

Teacher: Millie, give me a sentence starting with "I".

Millie: I is ...

Teacher: No, Millie. Always say, "I am".

Millie: All right, I am the ninth letter of the alphabet.

Agnes

Teacher: Paul, your composition on "My Dog" is exactly the same as your brother's. Did you copy his?

Paul: No, it's the same dog.

Agnes

Teacher: Harold, what do you call a person who keeps on talking when people are no longer interested?

Harold: A teacher.

Agnes

A wee boy came home after his first day at school.

"So what did you learn?" asked his mother.

"Not enough," said the wee boy. "They want
me back tomorrow."　　　　　　　　　　　　*Ed*

"Edward, give me two pronouns," said the English
teacher to a pupil who was not paying attention.

"Who, me?" replied Edward.　　　　　　　*Ed*

A teacher went to a prison to teach English to
the prisoners.

"OK," she said, "who can tell me what a sentence is?"

James

In aid of the SDWG supported by Comic Relief and Alzheimer Scotland

Teacher: Glenn, how do you spell "crocodile"?

Glenn: K-R-O-K-O-D-I-A-L.

Teacher: No, that's wrong.

Glenn: Maybe it is wrong, but you asked me how I spell it.

Agnes

Animal magic

There were two tigers walking along Sauchiehall Street one day.

One said to the other, "No many people about today, are there?"

James

Two butterflies were chatting.

One said, "I can't go to the dancing on Saturday night."

The other one said, "Oh no, why is that?"

The first butterfly replied, "Because it's a mothball."

James

Did you hear about the cowboy who bought a dachshund puppy?

Everyone kept telling him to "get a long little doggy."

James

A three-legged dog limped into a Western bar and said:

"I'm looking for the man who shot my paw."   *James*

_____

Two workmen had just laid a new carpet and then noticed a bump in the middle.

"It must be my fags," Tom said, "and I can't be bothered to lift the carpet again so I'll just stamp it down."

He jumped on the carpet until it was flat.

Just then the lady of the house came through with some tea.

"Have you seen my hamster?" she asked.

James

Q: What do you get if you feed lemon to a cat?

A: A sour puss.

James

Baby skunk: "Mummy, can I have a chemistry set for my birthday?"

Mummy skunk: "What, and stink the house out?" *James*

A man went into a pet shop to buy a pet and after looking at several different animals came out with a centipede in a box.

When he got home he thought it would be nice to go out for a pint, so he opened the box and asked the centipede if he would like to take a walk to the local pub for a pint.

No answer.

"Would you like to walk to the pub for a pint?"
he asked more loudly than before.

Still no answer.

"I said would you like to walk to the pub for a pint?"
he shouted.

"Keep your hair on," the centipede finally replied,
"I'm just putting my shoes on."

The Rovers

Kids' jokes

The following jokes were sent in by P5, P6 and P7 pupils of Cross Arthurlie Primary School, Barrhead, East Renfrewshire

A man took his dog to the vet because the dog went squint-eyed.

The vet said he'd have to put it down.

"Just because he's got a squint?" asked the dog owner.

"No," said the vet, "because he's too heavy."

There was a party at the graveyard last night and everyone was dying to get in.

"Doctor, doctor, I think I've got a strawberry stuck to my head!"

"Oh good, I think I've got some cream for it!"

―――――――――

My pal's not so bright.

He was out with a couple of mates and they came to a magic slide.

Whatever you shouted as you went down, you landed in at the bottom.

His first mate shouted G O L D!

And his other pal shouted S I L V E R!

But my pal forgot himself and shouted

W E E ... !

There are two packets of crisps walking down the road.

A taxi stops and says, "Do you want a lift?"

The crisps say, "No thanks, we are walkers."

A man walks into a fishmonger's with a salmon under his arm.

He asks the fishmonger if he does fish cakes.

The fishmonger replies "Yes."

"Good," says the man. "It's his birthday."

Q: What did the Mummy ghost say to her baby on the car journey?

A: Fasten your sheetbelt!

Q: Why did the skeleton go to the BBQ?

A: Because it wanted some ribs.

———————————

Q: What's the strongest fish in the sea?

A: A mussel.

———————————

Q: What do you call a donkey with three legs?

A: A wonkey!

———————————

Q: What is King Kong's favourite football team?

A: Aston Gorilla.

Q: What did one traffic light say to the other?

A: Don't look now, I'm flashing.

———————————

Q: What did the tie say to the hat?

A: I'll hang about here and you go on ahead!

———————————

Q: What happened to the frog that broke down?

A: It got toad away!

———————————

Q: What do you call a man with leaves in his pocket?

A: Russell!

Q: What did the big chimney say to the baby chimney?

A: Stop smoking.

Q: What do you call a duster and an onion?

A: Tickled onion.

Q: Why couldn't the skeleton go to the dance?

A: Because he had no body to go with.

Q: What do you call a person dancing in the sink?

A: A tap dancer!

Q: What can a female giraffe have that no other animal can have?

A: A baby giraffe.

_____

Q: Did you hear about the magic tractor?

A: It turned into a field.

_____

Q: Why can't Cinderella play football?

A: Because her coach turned into a pumpkin!

_____

Q: Why did the orange stop rolling down the road?

A: Because it ran out of juice!

Q: What do you say about a no-eyed dinosaur?

A: Do you think he sau-rus?

Q: What do you call a spider with no legs?

A: A raisin.

Q: What do you call a witch on the sand?

A: A sandwich.

Q: How do you start a teddy bear race?

A: Ready, Teddy, Go!

Q: Why did the golfer take 2 pairs of trousers?

A: In case he got a hole in one!

Q: What do you call a French man wearing sandals?

A: Phillipe Felop.

Q: What is black and white and rolls down a hill?

A: A penguin.

Q: What room do ghosts avoid?

A: A living room.

Q: What did the ocean say to the other ocean?

A: Nothing. They just waved.

Q: There are 10 copycats on a ship. One fell overboard. How many copy cats are left on the ship?

A: None.

Q: What do cows do at the weekend?

A: Go to the moooovies.

Q: What do you call a man with a seagull on his head?

A: Cliff.   *Christopher McCloy — age 13*

Q: What do you call a famous person with biscuits on his head?

A: Lionel Richtea.

Christopher McCloy — age 13

John was studying his marriage certificate.

"What are you looking for darling," his wife says.

John replies, "I'm looking for the expiry date."

Christopher McCloy — age 13

A slight
technical hitch

A scientist was on his way to give yet another of his lectures when his chauffeur said, "I've heard that talk so many times I could give it myself."

"OK, why don't you do that," said the scientist, "and I will have a night off."

So the scientist wore the chauffeur's hat and sat at the back of the hall. The chauffeur gave a great talk but at the end was asked an awkward question.

"Ha," he said, "that's so easy I will let my chauffeur sitting at the back answer it."

James

Q: Why do scientists disable their doorbells?

A: Because they want to win the Nobel Prize.

James

Q: What's the best invention ever?

A: Venetian blinds. If it wasn't for them, it would be curtains for us all.

James

Q: What do you call an Underground train full of professors?

A: A tube of Smarties.

Ed

"Excuse me," said the man to the library assistant, "how do I get onto the computer?"

"Give me your name and wait," she said.

"I'm called Tom and my weight is 12 stone," he said.

James

In aid of the SDWG supported by Comic Relief and Alzheimer Scotland

An eminent professor went to the chemist's.

"Give me some acetylsalicylic tablets," he said.

"Do you mean aspirin?" the chemist asked.

"Yes," the professor replied, "I can never remember that name."

James

Attributed to UPS Airlines

Remember it takes a college degree to fly a plane, but only a high school diploma to fix one; a reassurance to those of us who fly routinely in our jobs.

After every flight, UPS pilots fill out a form, called a "gripe sheet", which tells mechanics about problems with the aircraft.

The mechanics correct the problems, document their repairs on the form, and then pilots review the gripe sheets before the next flight.

Never let it be said that ground crews lack a sense of humour.

Here are some actual maintenance complaints submitted by pilots (marked with a P) and the solutions recorded (marked with an S) by maintenance engineers.

P: Noise coming from under instrument panel. Sounds like a midget pounding on something with a hammer.

S: Took hammer away from midget.

P: Left inside main tyre almost needs replacement.

S: Almost replaced left inside main tyre.

P: DME volume unbelievably loud.

S: DME volume set to more believable level.

P: Evidence of leak on right main landing gear.

S: Evidence removed.

P: Test flight OK, except autoland very rough.

S: Autoland not installed on this aircraft.

P: Something loose in cockpit.

S: Something tightened in cockpit.

P: Number 3 engine missing.

S: Engine found on right wing after brief search.

P: Mouse in cockpit.

S: Cat installed.

P: Dead bugs on windshield.

S: Live bugs on back-order.

P: Autopilot in altitude-hold mode produces a 200 feet per minute descent.

S: Cannot reproduce problem on ground.

P: Friction locks cause throttle levers to stick.

S: That's what friction locks are for.

P: IFF inoperative in OFF mode.

S: IFF always inoperative in OFF mode.

P: Suspected crack in windshield.

S: Suspect you're right.

P: Aircraft handles funny.

S: Aircraft warned to straighten up, fly right and be serious.

A man walks
into a bar...

Two youthful hamburgers walked into a pub.

"Sorry, we don't serve food," the barman said.　*James*

A man walked into a pub with a piece of tarmac under his arm.

"A pint for me and one for the road," he said.　*James*

Three drunk men were walking through a forest when they came across a set of tracks.

"These are a fox's tracks," said one.

"No, they're a wild boar's," muttered another.

"They are definitely a deer's," said the third.

They were still arguing when a train hit them.　*James*

It's night and a couple are sleeping in bed when there's a knock on the front door.

The husband gets out of bed and hurries downstairs. He opens the door and finds a drunk waiting outside.

"Hey," says the man. "Be a pal and give me a push."

"No!" shouts the householder. "Do you know what time it is?"

He slams the door and goes back to bed, and explains what happened to his wife.

"You should be ashamed of yourself," says his wife. "That man was asking for help and you turned him down flat. Go and help him push his car."

Her husband gives in, puts on some clothes and goes down to the front door.

He opens it and calls out into the darkness, "Hey! Do you still want a push?"

"Yesh!" the drunk shouts back, "I'm over here on your swing!"

Kath

A man walked into a bar.

Ouch! It was an iron bar.   *James*

A drunk wanders into a Temperance meeting.

The preacher thunders about the evils of alcohol.

"Let me show you" he rants, pouring out a half of whisky and dropping a wriggling worm into the glass.

A minute later he lifts out the worm, stone-dead.

"Now," the preacher bellows, "what lesson do you take from that?"

The drunk at the back of the hall sticks up his hand.

"Sir," he says, "if you have worms, drink plenty of whisky."

James

Saints and sinners

A man is about to be savaged by an enormous bear. Terrified, he cries out, "God help me!"

A bright light appears in the sky and a voice booms, "Why should I help you when you've led a wicked life and never even believed in me?"

"I know, I'm sorry," says the man. "But I promise that I'll become a Christian if you save me."

"No," says God. "It's too late for you to change now."

"Well, could you at least make the bear a Christian?" begs the man.

"Fair enough," God replies.

The bright light disappears and the man notices the bear has fallen to its knees. Then it puts its hands together and says, "For what we are about to receive ..."

James

Saint Peter halted a man at the gates of heaven.

"You've told too many lies to be admitted here," he said.

Replied the man, "Have a heart — you were a fisherman once."

Ed

Did you hear about the Satanist who couldn't spell?

He sold his soul to Santa.

James

Q: Who is the fastest runner in history?

A: Adam, because he was first in the human race.   *James*

A man arrives at the Pearly Gates, waiting to be admitted. God is reading through the Big Book to see if the man's name is written in it.

After several minutes, God closes the book, furrows his brow and says, "I'm sorry, I don't see your name written in the Book."

"How current is your copy?" the man asks.

"I get a download every ten minutes," God replies. "Why do you ask?"

"I'm embarrassed to admit it, but I was always the stubborn type. It was not until my death was imminent that I cried out to you God, so my name probably hasn't arrived to your copy yet."

"I'm glad to hear that," God says, "but while we're waiting for the update to come through, can you tell me about a really good deed that you did in your life?"

The man thinks for a moment and says, "Humm, well there was this one time when I was driving down a road and I saw a giant group of biker-gang members harassing this poor girl.

"I slowed down, and sure enough, there they were, about 20 of them torturing this poor woman.

"Infuriated, I got out my car, grabbed a tyre iron out of my boot, and walked up to the leader of the gang.

"He was a huge guy; 6-foot-4, 260 pounds, with a studded leather jacket and a chain running from his nose to his ears.

"As I walked up to the leader, the bikers formed a circle around me and told me to get lost or I'd be next.

"So I ripped the leader's chain off his face and yelled to the rest of them saying, 'Leave this poor innocent girl alone! You're all a bunch of sickos! Go home before I really teach you a lesson!' "

God, duly impressed, says "Wow! When did this happen?"

"About three minutes ago."

In aid of the SDWG supported by Comic Relief and Alzheimer Scotland

There was a monastery in which the monks communicated by chanting, and each day they chanted "Good morning" to the abbot.

One day a monk chanted "Good evening" by mistake.

The abbot glared and said, "Someone chanted evening."

James

After sixty years as a monk, Brother Tom was asked to help with transcribing Holy Writ and queried how people knew it was correct. The abbot said that it had been copied down faithfully over the years, and gave him the original to study.

Later he found Brother Tom in tears.

"CeleBRATE, celeBRATE, that's the word," he moaned.

James

Church clangers

The sentences that follow, with all their amusing mistakes, actually appeared in Church bulletins or were announced in Church services.

The Fasting & Prayer Conference includes meals.

———————————

The sermon this morning: "Jesus Walks on the Water". The sermon tonight: "Searching for Jesus".

———————————

Ladies, don't forget the jumble sale. It's a chance to get rid of those things not worth keeping around the house. Bring your husbands.

Low Self-Esteem Support Group will meet Thursday at 7pm. Please use the back door.

———————————

Don't let worry kill you off — let the Church help.

———————————

Miss Charlene Mason sang "I will not pass this way again", giving obvious pleasure to the congregation.

———————————

For those of you who have children and don't know it, we have a nursery downstairs.

Next Thursday there will be tryouts for the choir. They need all the help they can get.

Irving Benson and Jessie Carter were married on October 24 in the Church. So ends a friendship that began in their schooldays.

A bean supper will be held on Tuesday evening in the Church Hall. Music will follow.

At the evening service tonight, the sermon topic will be "What Is Hell?"

Come early and listen to our choir practice.

Ladies Bible Study will be held Thursday morning at 10am. All ladies are invited to lunch in the Fellowship Hall after the B. S. is done.

———————————

Please place your donation in the envelope along with the deceased person you want remembered.

———————————

Eight new choir robes are currently needed due to the addition of several new members and to the deterioration of some older ones.

———————————

Scouts are saving aluminium cans, bottles and other items to be recycled. Proceeds will be used to cripple children.

The Church will host an evening of fine dining, super entertainment and gracious hostility.

―――――――――

Potluck supper Sunday at 5pm — prayer and medication to follow.

―――――――――

The ladies of the Church have cast off clothing of every kind. They may be seen in the basement on Friday afternoon.

―――――――――

The Assistant Minister unveiled the Church's new campaign slogan last Sunday: "I Upped My Pledge — Up Yours".

This evening at 7pm there will be hymn singing in the park across from the Church. Bring a blanket and come prepared to sin.

The pastor would appreciate it if the ladies of the congregation would lend him their electric girdles for the pancake breakfast next Sunday.

Remember in prayer the many who are sick of our community. Smile at someone who is hard to love. Say "Hell" to someone who doesn't care much about you.

The Youth Club will be presenting Shakespeare's Hamlet in the Church basement Friday at 7pm. The congregation is invited to attend this tragedy.

Weight Watchers will meet at 7pm at the First Presbyterian Church. Please use large double door at the side entrance.

Strong arm of the law

Did you hear about the man who was robbed in his own flower shop?

He was a petrified florist.

James

"What do you mean you have only one brother?" the judge asked the youth.

"Your sister has already testified under oath that she has two brothers!"

James

Thieves have stolen the toilets from the local police station.

A police spokesman says they have nothing to go on.

James

A man went to a seance and was annoyed when the psychic laughed at gullible people, so he punched her.

He was subsequently charged with striking a happy medium.

James

Q: Why was the man arrested for standing in the marquee?

A: He was loitering within tent.

James

A police officer made the mistake of arresting a judge who went to a fancy dress party dressed as a convict.

It taught him a lesson.

You should never book a judge by his cover.

James

Quasimodo attacked a girl in Paris, and when she went to the police station she was shown photographs to help identify her attacker. When she came to the one of Quasimodo she paused.

"Was that the man?" the gendarme asked.
"Do you know him?"

"No," she said, "but his face rings a bell."   *James*

Q: What happened to the man who threw bleach over the constable?

A: He was charged with bleach of police.   *James*

The following dialogues were taken from *Disorder in the Court* by Charles M. Sevilla.

Attorney: What was the first thing your husband said to you that morning?

Witness: He said, "Where am I, Cathy?"

Attorney: And why did that upset you?

Witness: My name is Susan!

———————————

Attorney: Doctor, how many of your autopsies have you performed on dead people?

Witness: All of them. The live ones put up too much of a fight.

Attorney: Which gear were you in at the moment of the impact?

Witness: Gucci sweats and Reeboks.

Attorney: She had three children, right?

Witness: Yes.

Attorney: How many were boys?

Witness: None.

Attorney: Were there any girls?

Witness: Your Honour, I think I need a different attorney. Can I get a new attorney?

Attorney: The youngest son, the twenty-year-old, how old is he?

Witness: He's twenty, much like your IQ.

Attorney: How was your first marriage terminated?

Witness: By death.

Attorney: And by whose death was it terminated?

Witness: Take a guess.

_____

Attorney: Can you describe the individual?

Witness: He was about medium height and had a beard.

Attorney: Was this a male or a female?

Witness: Unless the circus was in town I'm going with male.

Attorney: Doctor, before you performed the autopsy, did you check for a pulse?

Witness: No.

Attorney: Did you check for blood pressure?

Witness: No.

Attorney: Did you check for breathing?

Witness: No.

Attorney: So, then it is possible that the patient was alive when you began the autopsy?

Witness: No.

Attorney: How can you be so sure, Doctor?

Witness: Because his brain was sitting on my desk in a jar.

Attorney: I see, but could the patient have still been alive, nevertheless?

Witness: Yes, it is possible that he could have been alive and practising law.

Attorney: Are you qualified to give a urine sample?

Witness: Are you qualified to ask that question?

Attorney: Now doctor, isn't it true that when a person dies in his sleep, he doesn't know about it until the next morning?

Witness: Did you actually pass the bar exam?

Attorney: ALL your responses MUST be oral, OK?
What school did you go to?

Witness: Oral.

Attorney: Is your appearance here this morning pursuant to a deposition notice which I sent to your attorney?

Witness: No, this is how I dress when I go to work.

Attorney: Do you recall the time that you examined the body?

Witness: The autopsy started around 8:30pm.

Attorney: And Mr Denton was dead at the time?

Witness: If not, he was by the time I finished.

Cannibal capers

Did you hear about the cannibal student? He was suspended from school for buttering up his teacher.

James

Q: What is the title of the best-selling cannibal cookery book?

A: How to Serve Your Fellow Man.

James

Q: What do cannibals do at a wedding?

A: They toast the bride and groom.

James

Did you hear about the cannibal who was late
for the feast?

He got the cold shoulder.   *James*

Two cannibals were sitting at a table.

"Never met a human I didn't like," one said to
the other.   *James*

A missionary was once sent to convert cannibals.
They ate and enjoyed him but were violently
sick afterwards.

So it's true what they say: you can't keep a good
man down.   *James*

Two cannibals were sitting at the table feeling full.

"Your wife makes a good roast," said one.

"Yes," replied the other, "I will miss her."   *James*

_____

Q: Where does it cost £20 a head to eat?

A: A cannibal restaurant.   *James*

_____

Most cannibal jokes are in poor taste.   *James*

No laughing matter

Did you hear about the undertaker who buried someone in the wrong plot?

He was sacked for grave misconduct. *James*

―――――――――

A Frenchman was drowning in the River Clyde.

A wee Glasgow man, with the proverbial bunnet, pulled him into the rescue boat.

The appreciative Frenchman said, "Merci, merci."

The wee Glasgow man gave a shrug and threw him back into the Clyde again.

Frank McAveety, MSP

―――――――――

Sign at the entrance to a cemetery in the East Riding of Yorkshire: "One-way system in operation." *James*

A funeral service is being held for a woman who has just passed away.

At the end of the service, the pall-bearers are carrying the coffin out when they accidentally bump into a wall, jarring the coffin. They hear a faint moan.

They open the coffin and find that the woman is actually alive!

She lives for ten more years, and then dies.

Once again, a ceremony is held, and at the end of it, the pall-bearers are again carrying out the coffin.

As they carry it towards the door, her widower cries out, "Watch that wall!"

Chris McGregor, Vice-Convener, Alzheimer Scotland

"I tried to kill myself by taking 100 aspirins yesterday."

"What happened?"

"Well, after taking two I felt much better."   *James*

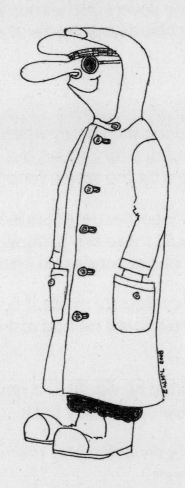

The Rovers

The true stories in this section have been
sent in by The Rovers, Alzheimer Scotland,
South Aberdeenshire Services.

After a night out during the winter when there was lots
of snow on the ground, a farmer set out on the long
country road home a bit the worse for drink.

As both he and the weather deteriorated he soon found
the only way he could make any progress through the
snow was to crawl on his hands and knees.

In this manner, he eventually made it back to his warm
fireside only to discover that he had lost his false teeth
on the journey.

Reluctantly he decided he would just have to do an
about-turn and crawl all the way back.

He reckons he has been looking for them ever since but
still hasn't found them.

After a family wedding a man invited some of his fellow guests back to his house for a nightcap. On arrival at the house, however, he remembered that he had given the key to his daughter, who was still back at the wedding reception.

So as not to keep his guests waiting out in the cold, he decided to go round to the back of the house where he could use a ladder to get in through the open bedroom window and go down to open the door to let the others in.

After much huffing and puffing, he reached the bedroom window only to be met by his daughter.

When he went down to the living room everyone else was already there enjoying a drink.

"It wound roond ma hert like a big hairy worm" — a description of a particularly good plate of thick steaming Scotch broth.

On one occasion a plane landed on the runway at Heathrow at such a speed and with such a bang that some of the passengers actually screamed.

Once they had taxied to a halt, however, the captain's cheery voice came on the intercom to announce, "That's another early arrival for Ryanair!"

Quiz time

Q: What did the mother turkey say to her son?

A: If your father could see you now, he would turn over in his gravy.

James

_____

Q: What's the difference between a sick horse and a dead bee?

A: One is a sickly beast and the other is a bee deceased.

James

_____

Q: Why did the chicken run on to the football field?

A: Because the referee blew for a fowl.

James

Q: What's black and white and goes round and round?

A: A zebra stuck in a revolving door.　　　　　*James*

———————————

Q: Why are soldiers so tired on the 1st of April?

A: They just had a 31-day March.　　　　　*James*

———————————

Q: What do home-brewed beer and a boat have in common?

A: They're both near to water.　　　　　*James*

Q: How do you get down from an elephant?

A: You don't, you get down from a duck.   *James*

———————————

Q: What happened to the survivors of a collision between a ship carrying red paint and a ship carrying blue paint?

A: They were marooned.   *James*

———————————

Q: Why did the raisin go out with the prune?

A: Because he couldn't find a date.   *James*

Q: Why did the tomato blush?

A: Because it saw the salad dressing.   *James*

Q: What happened to the two bedbugs who fell in love?

A: They married in the spring.   *James*

Q: How can you drop an egg three feet without breaking it?

A: Drop it four feet. For the first three feet the egg will not hit anything.   *Agnes's nephew*

Q: What's green, covered in custard and unhappy?

A: Apple grumble. *James*

Q: Why did the orange visit the doctor?

A: Because it wasn't peeling very well. *James*

Q: What's worse than biting into an apple and finding a worm?

A: Finding half a worm. *James*

Q: From what number can you take half and leave nothing?

A: The number 8. Take away the top half and 0 is left.

Agnes's nephew

Q: What do you get if you cross an egg white with gunpowder?

A: A boom meringue.

James

Q: What did the parents say when their son asked for a drum kit?

A: Beat it.

James

Q: How do monkeys get down the stairs?

A: Using the banana-stairs.   *Heather*

Q: How do you make an apple puff ?

A: Chase it around the garden.

Q: What is the quickest cake in the world?

A: Scone.   *Bob Doris, MSP*

Q: What do you get if you cross a door-knocker with a courgette?

A: Rat-a-tat-a-touille.   *Ed*

Q: What were the names of two Mexican fire-fighting brothers?

A: Hose-A and Hose-B.   *Ed*

Q: How can you make a fire with only one stick?

A: Easy. Just make sure it's a matchstick.   *Agnes's nephew*

Q: How should you treat a baby goat?

A: Like a kid.

Agnes's nephew

Q: Is it better to say, "The yolk of an egg is white", or "The yolk of an egg are white"?

A: Neither. An egg yolk is yellow.

Agnes's nephew

Q: What is the best birthday present?

A: It's hard to say, but a drum takes a lot of beating.

James

Q: Is it better to write on a full or on an empty stomach?

A: Neither. Paper is much better.   *Agnes's nephew*

———————————————

Q: What bus crossed the ocean?

A: Christopher Columbus.   *Agnes's nephew*

———————————————

Q: Who is the patron saint of slimmers?

A: Saint Gabriel — he came down to announce.
                    Alzheimer Scotland, Aberdeen City Services, Drop In

Q: What do you call a cow that goes on holiday?

A: A wee calf.   *Alex Salmond, First Minister*

―――――――――――

Q: What do you call a man who is nearly home?

A: Hamish.   *Alex Salmond, First Minister*

―――――――――――

Q: Why did the toilet roll run down the hill?

A: To get to the bottom.   *Heather*

Lucky dip

There was a young man of Devizes

Whose ears were different sizes;

One was so small

It was no use at all,

The other won several prizes.

James

"I went to a party last night and we played Jockey Knock."

"What's that?"

"It's like Postman's Knock, only with more horseplay."

Ed

A man dressed as a pair of jump leads went to a fancy dress party.

The host said, "Come in, as long as you don't start anything."

James

———————————

A man fell asleep on the couch watching football on TV. His wife woke him in the morning and said, "It's seven fifteen."

"In whose favour?" asked her husband.

James

———————————

A cowboy got off his horse, lifted its tail and kissed its bum.

"Why did you do that?" asked a passerby.

"Well, I've got chapped lips," said the cowboy, "and it stops me from licking them."

James

Two boll weevil brothers parted company. One went to Hollywood and became a famous star. The other stayed at home and amounted to nothing. He became known as the lesser of two weevils.

James

A tourist was going round Nelson's flagship, HMS Victory. The guide pointed to a brass plaque on the deck and said, "That's where Nelson fell."

"I'm not surprised," the tourist said, "I tripped on the damn thing myself."

James

Two atoms ran into each other. "Oh dear," said one, "I think I've lost an electron."

"Are you sure?" the other said.

"Yes, I'm positive," said the first.

James

Velcro — what a rip off!   *Tim Vine*

A boat attendant at the pond shouted, "Come in, number 9, your time is up!"

"We only have eight boats," said his assistant.

"Oh dear," said the attendant, "number 6 must be in trouble."   *James*

I was at the theatre and two ladies in front of me chatted non-stop. I tapped one on the shoulder and said, "Excuse me, I can't hear."

"I should hope not," she replied. "This is a private conversation."   *James*

A man came out of Buckingham Palace covered in wallpaper and emulsion.

A policeman said, "What has happened to you?"

The man replied, "I've just been decorated by the Queen."

James

Ticket seller: "That's the fifth ticket you've bought, sir."

Cinema-goer: "I know, but the girl inside keeps tearing them up."

James

A man was doing a crossword. His pal leant over and said, "I don't know what 6 down is but 7 up's lemonade."

Tim Vine

Exit signs — they're on the way out!   *Tim Vine*

———————

When God gave out noses I thought he said roses

So I asked for a big bright red one!   *Shona*

———————

I never forget a face, but I'll make an exception
in your case.   *Groucho Marx; sent in by Christopher Harvie, MSP*

———————

Three tomatoes were walking down the street —
Mummy tomato, Daddy tomato and Baby tomato.

Baby tomato was lagging behind and Daddy tomato
turned around and says "Ketchup!"   *Heather*

A woman was about to do a parachute jump for charity and the instructor said to pull the cord at 300 feet.

"How will I know when I am at 300 feet?" she asked.

"Well," the instructor said, "at that height you can recognise the faces of people on the ground."

"What if there is nobody I recognise?" she asked.   *James*

What is the difference between a rich Scotsman, a poor Scotsman and a dead Scotsman?

A rich Scotsman has a canopy over his bed.

A poor Scotsman has a can o' pee under his bed.

And a dead Scotsman canna pee at all.

Professor June Andrews, Dementia Services Development Centre, University of Stirling

Murphy's lesser-known laws

1. Light travels faster than sound. This is why some people appear bright until you hear them speak.

    _____

2. Change is inevitable, except from a vending machine.

    _____

3. Those who live by the sword get shot by those who don't.

    _____

4. Nothing is foolproof to a sufficiently talented fool.

5. The 50–50–90 rule: any time you have a 50–50 chance of getting something right, there's a 90 per cent probability you'll get it wrong.

———————————

6. If you lined up all the cars in the world end to end, someone would be stupid enough to try to pass them.

———————————

7. The things that come to those who wait will be the scraggy junk left by those who got there first.

———————————

8. The shin bone is a device for finding furniture in a dark room.

9. A fine is a tax for doing wrong. A tax is a fine for doing well.

_____

10. When you go into court, you are putting yourself into the hands of twelve people who weren't smart enough to get out of jury duty.

Chris McGregor, Vice-Convener, Alzheimer Scotland

About the SDWG

The Scottish Dementia Working Group (SDWG) was formed in 2002 by a group of people with a diagnosis of dementia who wanted to speak for themselves. The SDWG is an independent group run by people with dementia under the umbrella of Alzheimer Scotland.

The SDWG aims to:

- Be the voice of and for people with dementia in Scotland

- Influence public policies that impact on the lives of people with dementia and their families

- Promote improved provision of services

- Develop information, education, awareness and training

- Reduce the prejudice and stigma attached to dementia.

As far as we are aware, the SDWG is the only group worldwide that has been established purely as a national campaigning group.

Currently there are 85 members across Scotland.

The SDWG Committee meets every two months to conduct business. Ordinary meetings, to which all members are invited, are held in Glasgow every two months, and in Dundee, also every two months.

Since its formation, the SDWG has achieved considerable success in achieving its aims.

The SDWG has:

• Campaigned on medical issues and respite care among other things

Currently, one area we are campaigning on is to raise awareness of the visual difficulties associated with dementia.

Many people with dementia have problems with vision and perception, which can have an enormous impact on their lives, but awareness of the particular difficulties they and their carers face is very low.

• Met with ministers and other politicians

The SDWG meets with the Minister for Public Health at least annually, which provides a valuable opportunity to raise issues at government level.

• Submitted views to a wide range of organisations

The SDWG regularly takes part in consultations on a wide range of matters.

• Played an active role in Alzheimer Scotland

The SDWG as the voice of people with dementia is much valued by Alzheimer Scotland. Members are represented on the organisation's Council and standing committees and can therefore directly influence its direction.

•Produced two DVDs – with a third on the way

Listening to the Experts is widely used as a training tool and *United We Stand* is a very useful promotional tool in tackling people's attitudes towards dementia.

A new training DVD, *Through Our Eyes — A Life with Dementia,* will be available from June 2010. It is anticipated that this will become an important resource in the training of professionals.

• Worked with the Scottish Government in a number of key areas

The Scottish Government is currently developing a Dementia Strategy, which will shape the future provision of dementia services in Scotland. Members of the SDWG were represented on each of the five workstreams who worked on the development of the Strategy, and the SDWG was a partner in running the consultation on the draft recommendations. The Dementia Strategy was launched on 1 June 2010.

• Spoken at conferences in Scotland and abroad

Members have spoken at numerous conferences across the UK and Europe and further afield, including Singapore, Istanbul, Beirut and the Dominican Republic.

These talks, with members speaking about both their personal experiences and the wider needs of people with dementia, are always inspirational and often very moving, conveying a powerful message.

• Contributed to the professional training of student social workers, doctors and nurses

These sessions have a tremendous impact and feedback is always very positive. Members are told that "hearing someone talking from experience is better than dozens of lectures from people who know the textbooks but don't have the experience."

Although the SDWG was established as a campaigning group, an important role of the group is to bring people with a diagnosis of dementia together to gain support from each other.

Being a member of the SDWG has had a dramatic effect on many people and below are just a few quotes that clearly demonstrate the positive impact of being part of the group:

"In 2005 I had the opportunity to do a presentation at the Alzheimer's Disease International conference in Istanbul. That was a great experience and really gave me confidence. A few years earlier I would never have stood up in front of an audience and spoken, but I've done it a lot since I joined SDWG. I've spoken in Glasgow, York, Oxford and several other places. I've helped with research and been on the advisory group for research on Talking Mats in the University of Stirling's Department of Psychology."

"Being part of the Scottish Dementia Working Group was my introduction back into society, the first step on a journey and a new beginning, living with dementia. I met other people with dementia. They helped me manage my daily problems. They were the only people who made me feel safe and that I belonged. They gave me my confidence back."

"Karen got me involved with the Scottish Dementia Working Group, and the group gave me a challenge and this was what I needed to get me out of bed each

morning, to iron a shirt and slacks. I am very proud
to be part of the Scottish Dementia Working Group.
It has given me and many others a new confidence.
As a campaigning group it is an outstanding success
and doing Scotland proud."

Some more quotes from members of the SDWG about having dementia

"I expect as much respect for myself as you expect for
yourself. I have a problem with memory and recall. I
have not misplaced my sense of dignity nor lost my
ability to respect others."

––––––––––––––––––

"I hope you will see me functioning at a high level. But
don't underestimate what I do behind the scenes to
pull this off. I don't really think anyone can appreciate
the subtleties if they do not have the diagnosis."

"I am a person, not an illness. I've told my care workers I'm not a number, I have a name. I'm a person."

———————

"To me, it's all down to determination — get on with your life, and make the most of what you've got."

———————

"I think I now have a greater freedom to say exactly what I think. That inner voice that used to stop me doesn't whisper so loudly now!"

"Personally, I would not like to go back to not having dementia. I'm now in love with dementia and fascinated with the condition. I now understand how a kaleidoscope works. Shake me and find out!"

———————

"I described having dementia like being a swan — you look OK on the surface but your legs are going like crazy to keep you afloat."

———————

"People with dementia can be thoroughly discombobulated and the quicker they can get back to some form of normality the better."

"Openness pays off. There's no point in trying to disguise it. Determination is important, just as it is for anybody else."

———————

"Your own positive attitude towards the problem is the most important. If you take the bull by the horns and challenge dementia head-on you're half way there."

———————

"People don't openly say what they think in case you might be upset. I like to be given it on the chin."

"I'd like to change peoples' views about dementia. Then we could be included normally. Integration is the key to being accepted as a full member of society."

———————————

"IT WAS UP TO US. So I, and others, got the idea that if we wanted change, we had to do it ourselves."

———————————

"People with dementia can not only be capable of advocating for themselves but can band together to form their own advocacy groups, to be able to run them with a modicum of support and to clamour to the powers that be, for recognition and respect. We must earn that respect by our actions."

"Did professionals have low expectations of us? Was it not the done thing? Could we not be trusted to have our own groups? What did they fear, if people with dementia got together?"

———————————

"There is a lot of talk about the stigma of dementia. We believe we can do something about it. By hiding our diagnosis we help to create the stigma. The people creating the stigma are ourselves because we are ashamed of the condition."

———————————

"As well as empowering ourselves by finding answers and roads out of despair, we should also empower professional workers and explain to them that there is life after dementia."

Who to contact

SDWG

Tel: 0141 418 3939

Email: sdwg@alzscot.org

Web: www.sdwg.org.uk

Dementia Helpline

For more information or to talk things over confidentially with someone who understands call the free Dementia Helpline: 0808 808 3000. The Helpline is open 24 hours a day every day of the year.

Acknowledgements

The Scottish Dementia Working Group would like to thank all our members and supporters who have contributed jokes to *Why am I laughing?*

This book has been produced with Waverley Books, publisher of *Maw Broon's Cookbook*, to raise awareness about dementia.

The sale of this book will also raise funds for the Scottish Dementia Working Group.